I0693663

Thank you to all the teachers that inspired you to
become a teacher.

Children learn best when they like their teacher and they
think their teacher likes them.

"If at first you don't succeed, try, try again."

"Put your hand up if you want to speak."

"I'm counting 5,4,3,2,1."

"Last time I remember looking, I was the teacher."

"I can wait all day if that's what it takes."

"There's no such thing as can't."

"I believe in you."

"You'll get there in the end."

“I'm so proud of you.”

"See, I told you that you could do it."

"A little bit of effort goes a long way."

"You're smarter than you think."

“Don't let me have to ring your parents.”

"It doesn't matter what time it is get on with your work."

"I hope you washed your hands while you were in the toilet."

"For every minute you waste of your time that will be a minute off your playtime."

"You can have a sticker."

"You are my star of the week."

"Nobody leaves the classroom until we find the top to this glue stick."

"I'm not laughing!"

"Who put you in charge?"

"Never mind what he's doing get on with your work."

"I'm asking the questions around here."

“If he told you to jump off a cliff would you?”

"It's your time you're wasting not mine."

"Stand up straight like soldiers."

"Let's see who can walk as quietly as a mouse."

"I wish I was having a school dinner today."

"Sit up straight and smart and let's see who's ready to go."

“123 look at me, 456 my eyes are fixed.”

"Let's see who's table can be the first to tidy up."

"Let's see who's the first table to tidy up."

"I've got eyes in the back of my head you know."

"You wouldn't make that mess at home I'm sure."

"I'm not going to keep repeating myself, now do as you are told."

"Let's show the other classes how smart we are."

"I'm getting tired of repeating myself."

"Am I speaking a different language or are you just not listening?"

"If I have to ring you mum and dad they won't be impressed."

"I'm so proud of how hard you've tried this lesson."

"This time next year you'll be a genius."

“Is it me or can I hear someone talking?”

"Well by the level of noise in here some of you will be spending your playtime doing the work."

"It's my birthday today I bet no.one can guess how old I am?

"I'm not that old thank you very much."

"No, I wasn't around when dinosaurs were alive."

"Teachers don't go home they sleep at school."

"Teachers are allowed to have a life beyond school you know."

"What will I be doing this evening........marking and
planning your work."